Communicate!

How You Say It

Dona Herweck Rice

Publishing Credits

Rachelle Cracchiolo, *M.S.Ed., Publisher*
Conni Medina, *M.A.Ed., Managing Editor*
Nika Fabienke, *Ed.D., Series Developer*
June Kikuchi, *Content Director*
John Leach, *Assistant Editor*
Kevin Pham, *Graphic Designer*

TIME For Kids and the TIME For Kids logo are registered trademarks of TIME Inc. Used under license.

Image Credits: All images from iStock and/or Shutterstock.

Library of Congress Cataloging-in-Publication Data

Names: Rice, Dona, author.
Title: Communicate! : How you say it / Dona Herweck Rice.
Description: Huntington Beach, CA : Teacher Created Materials, [2017] | Series: Time for kids
Identifiers: LCCN 2017026883 (print) | LCCN 2017029754 (ebook) | ISBN 9781425853310 (eBook) | ISBN 9781425849573 (pbk.)
Subjects: LCSH: Communication--Juvenile literature.
Classification: LCC P91.2 (ebook) | LCC P91.2 .R43 2017 (print) | DDC 302.2--dc23
LC record available at https://lccn.loc.gov/2017026883

Teacher Created Materials

5301 Oceanus Drive
Huntington Beach, CA 92649-1030
http://www.tcmpub.com

ISBN 978-1-4258-4957-3

What is the best way to
say something?
The right words depend on
where you are.
They also depend on who
is around you.

What if something does not make sense?

With friends you may say,
"I don't get it."
With your teacher you
may say, "I do not
understand."

What if you **dislike** a strange food you just tasted?

With friends you may say,
"Yuck!"
With your family you may
say, "I do not care for
this."

What if you are
running late?

With friends you may say,
"Come on!"
With your father you may
say, "We should go now."

What if something new makes you happy?

With friends you may say,
"How cool!"
With your teacher you
may say, "That is really
great!"

What if you need to use
the restroom?

At home you may say, "I really have to go!"
With your teacher you may ask, "May I please use the restroom?"

What if something makes
you **frustrated**?

With friends you may say,
"Help!"
With your mother you
may say, "Please help
me."

What if you see someone laugh as they look at a computer **screen**?

With friends you may say,
"Let me see!"
With your father you may
ask, "May I look?"

What if you do not hear
what someone said?

With friends you may ask, "What?"
With your teacher you may ask, "Will you please repeat that?"

What if you meet someone
for the first time?

You may say, "Hi," when the person is your age. When you meet an **adult**, you may say, "It is nice to meet you."

You can choose the right words each time you speak.

That is your word
superpower!

Glossary

adult

dislike

frustrated

screen